BOOK 1
WRITTEN FOR YOU
PIANO SOLO COLLECTION

**Early Elementary/
Elementary Piano**

FEATURING ORIGINAL COMPOSITIONS BY
FOUR OUTSTANDING COMPOSERS

RECOMMENDED TEACHING TIPS
AND PRACTICE GUIDE BY
Yeeseon Kwon

CONTENTS

Recommended Teaching and Practice Guide

by Yeeseon Kwon

The ***Preparation*** suggestions are intended for use by teachers to motivate and musically prepare the student for each piece. Questions are posed to spark the student's imagination and reinforce the understanding of musical form, character, and expression.

The ***Student Practice Guide*** is designed to highlight and prepare musical and technical challenges in the piece. Teachers are encouraged to use the guide to effectively address specific practice steps. These guidelines should be demonstrated during the lesson, and teachers should encourage students to apply these practice steps at home. Guidelines for rhythm, technique, and expressive playing are included for students to model. Students are also asked to identify and mark areas of focus in the music for further exploration.

The varied styles and sounds of these appealing pieces will provide fun and motivation at the piano, while developing the technical and musical fundamentals of reading, rhythm, and expression. The pieces in the collection are compiled to progress gradually from the early elementary to the elementary level.

Wind Through the Trees *(page 6)*

Preparation

- Play the piece, while singing the words, and have the student sway to the music.
- Ask the student to identify characteristics of the wind. How do these characteristics relate to the music?
- Have the student circle all the dynamic marks in the piece.

Student Practice Guide

- Tap the piece hands together while counting aloud.
- Listen for smooth, connected sounds between the hands and project the melody evenly. Be sure to avoid any accents.
- Measure 33: Practice gradually slowing down while playing softer to create an expressive ending.
- Sing and play the piece smoothly.

In the Deep Blue "C" *(page 9)*

Preparation

- Ask what is "unusual" about the title.
- Have the student point out the return of the initial theme. (Measure 33) Where does it change?
- Have the student tap the rhythm pattern of the melody hands together in measures 1–8.

Reading Activity:

- Have the student find a measure that contains only 2nds. (Measures 2, 4, 34, or 36)
- Circle the two measures where the L.H. plays harmonic 3rds. (Measures 29 and 31)

Student Practice Guide

- Tap the piece hands together while counting aloud.
- Be sure to prepare and practice the R.H. movement at measures 31–33.
- Measures 9–12: Practice blocking the hands together on beat 1 of each measure, to reinforce directional reading and legato playing.
- Sing and play the piece smoothly.

Tropical Breezes *(page 12)*

Preparation

- Play the pieces while singing the words with the student.
- Have the student sway or rock gently to the music with a feeling of one beat to a measure.
- Discuss the similar characteristics of the tide, sea breeze, and sails. How do they musically relate to the piece?

Student Practice Guide

- Play and listen for a smooth, connected sound between the hands.
- Shape the phrases expressively in a long line, lifting the wrist gently to taper the phrases.
- Be sure the melodic lines flow with a feeling of one beat per measure in the first two pieces.

Sweet Dreams *(page 18)*

Preparation

- Discuss what dreams or images come to mind after hearing the piece.
- Which two lines begin differently from all the others?
- Have the student mark the form. (A A' B A")

Reading Activity:

- Have the student trace the left- and right-hand lines in the music to reinforce directional reading.
- Compare the parallel motion of the hands in measures 6–7 with measures 14–15.
- Have the student circle the L.H. crossover in the final measure.

Student Practice Guide

- Practice measures 17–25 first without pedal. Listen for a smooth, connected sound.
- Use a slight circular arm gesture in the R.H. in measures 1–2 to crescendo through the ascending 3-note figure before gently tapering the phrase.
- Practice pacing the two ritardandos gracefully.

Dancing Donkey (page 20)

Preparation

- Play the F-sharp and G together in different registers of the piano and ask the student to describe the sound.
- Have the student block other "half step" clusters built on black-white keys.
- Ask how the composer uses this sound for a "special effect" in this piece. What does this sound remind you of?
- Discuss and mark the places where the hands shift to higher and lower octaves. (Measures 33 and 51)
- Have the student mark the form.

Student Practice Guide

- Tap the rhythm and articulation in measures 4–8 hands together. Be sure to release the left hand lightly for the staccato effect.
- Listen for a smooth, connected line in the opening phrase. Maintain a round hand shape for projecting the melody expressively.
- Practice shaping the melodic phrase at measures 17 and 25 with a slight crescendo and diminuendo.
- Prepare and practice the R.H. crossover in the last two measures. The final "C" should be played firmly with a curved 3rd finger. Imagine hearing the donkey's final, emphatic step.

Grandfather's Grandfather Clock (page 24)

Preparation

- Discuss how the clock is musically depicted.
- What does one hear happening at measures 19 and 39?
- Play the piece while the student marks the form.

Student Practice Guide

- Practice the L.H. alone with the pedal in measures 19–26. Listen for smooth and clear changes of harmony.
- At measures 19 and 39, maintain a round hand position using the weight of the arm for a full and resonant tone without striking the keys.
- Listen for an even and steady rhythm throughout.
- Maintain a crisp, light staccato sound to depict the ticking clock. Keep the hands positioned close to the keys for even control of sound and dynamics.

The Hermit Crab Cha-Cha (page 27)

Preparation

- Have the student say the words "cha-cha-cha" in the rhythm of measures 1–3.
- What instruments can one imagine playing at measures 1 and 27? At measure 9?
- Have the student mark the form.

Student Practice Guide

- Tap hands together while counting aloud for rhythmic clarity.
- Play the thirds in the R.H. in rhythm as a warm-up to the piece.
- Prepare and practice a smooth transition in the L.H. at measures 26–27.
- Prepare and practice the R.H. shift to the higher octave in measures 25 to 27.
- Keep the fingers curved with a round hand shape when playing thirds in either hand.
- Keep the staccatos light and rhythmically even throughout.

Olde English Dance (page 30)

Preparation

- Discuss how the slur-staccato articulation in measures 1–2 contributes to the graceful and lilting character.
- Demonstrate and have the student listen to the gentle, musical "lift" effect of the staccato notes.
- Play the R.H. and have the student model the sound and articulation with the L.H. Do the phrases sound the same? Be sure to play in different registers of the piano and switch parts.
- Demonstrate how the hands smoothly follow and lead each other through the mirrored phrases, similar to partners in a dance.
- Discuss how many times the melodic pattern of measures 1–4 appears in the piece and how it is varied.

Student Practice Guide

- Block all the notes for each crossover pattern and smoothly practice the hand shifts.
- Lift the arm gently while playing the second staccato quarter note for a light, tapered effect in the opening motive.
- Taper the motive in each hand with a decrescendo for expressive phrasing.
- Listen carefully to avoid accenting the first note of each measure.
- Observe and practice the L.H. thumb crossing at measures 47–48. Prepare the thumb for a smooth motion toward measure 48.
- Play with a feeling of one beat per measure for a buoyant and stately character.

Wind Through the Trees

Timothy Brown

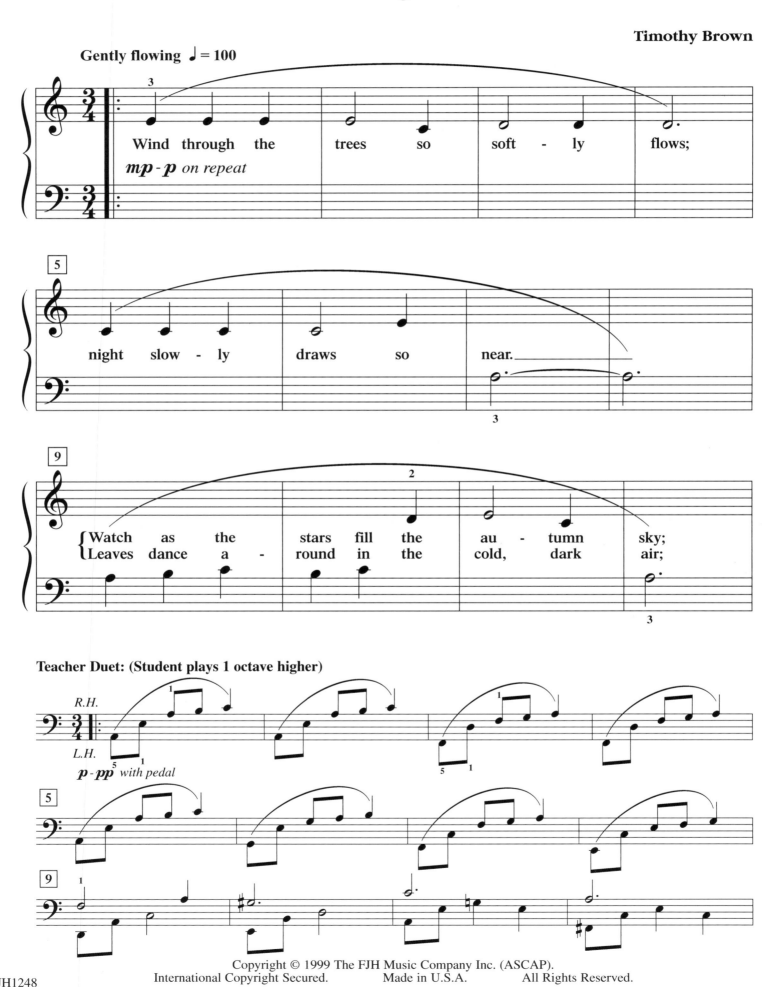

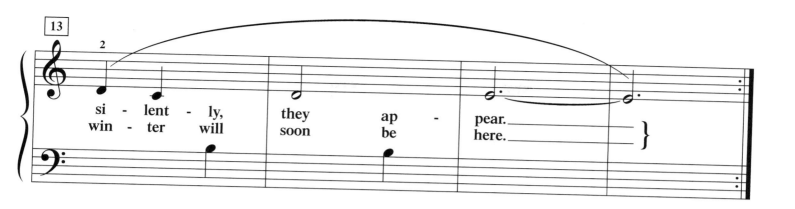

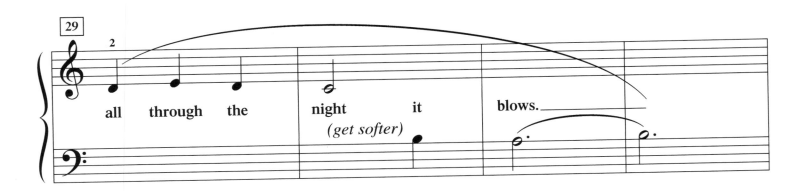

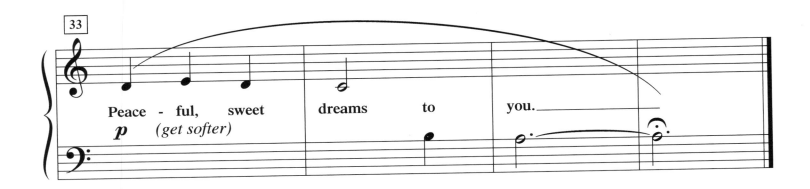

In the Deep Blue "C"

Kevin Olson

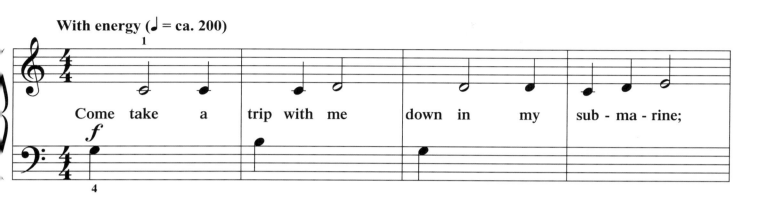

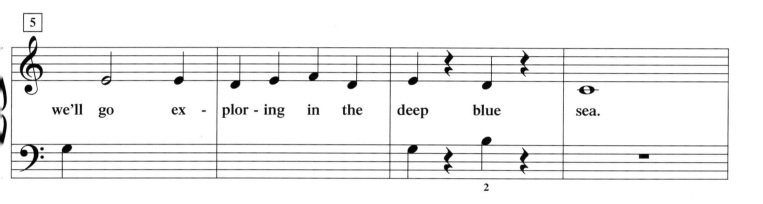

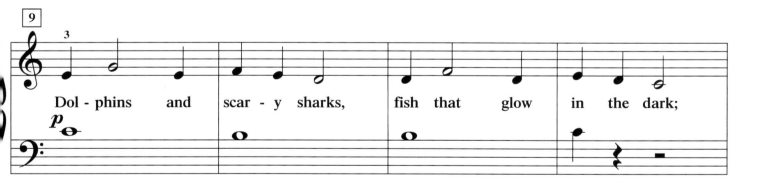

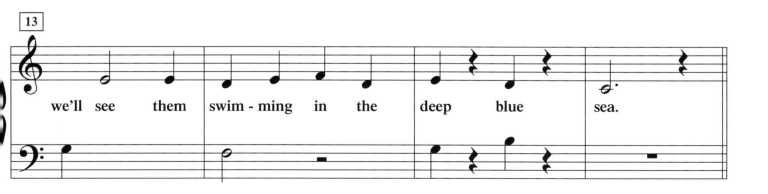

FJH1248

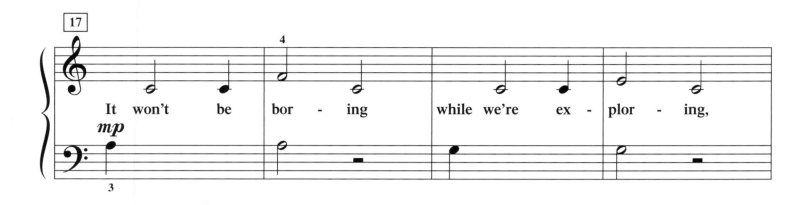

It won't be bor - ing while we're ex - plor - ing,

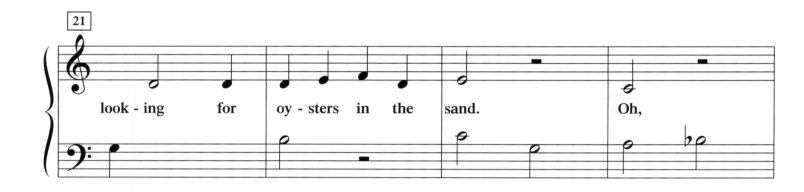

look - ing for oy - sters in the sand. Oh,

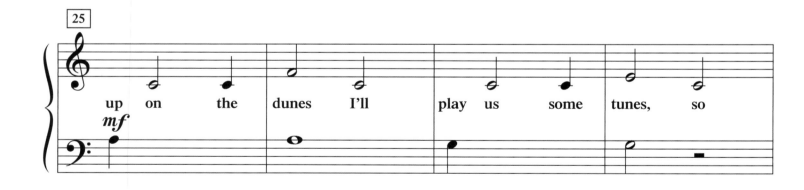

up on the dunes I'll play us some tunes, so

1 octave higher   *2 octaves higher*

don't for - get to bring the grand pi - a - no, oh, oh...

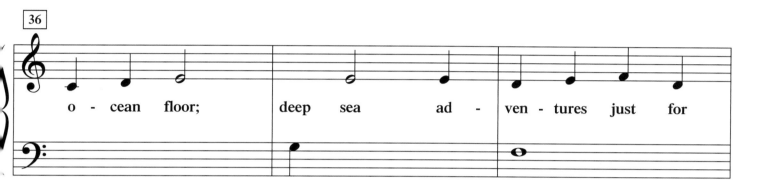

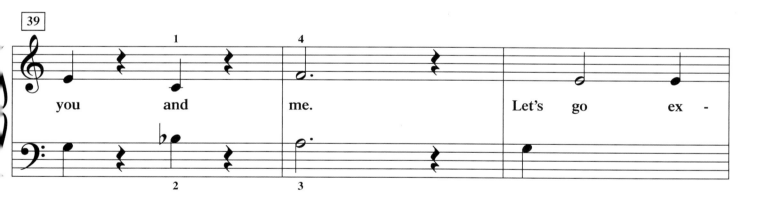

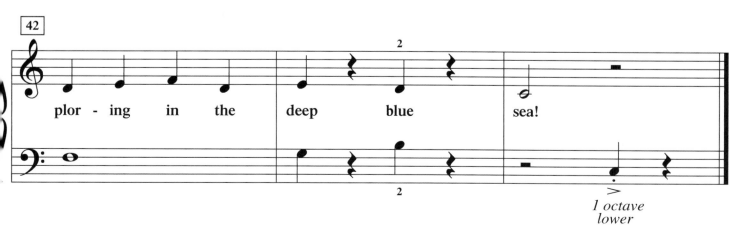

Tropical Breezes

Music by Timothy Brown
Lyrics by Roybeth Savage

Tropical Tide

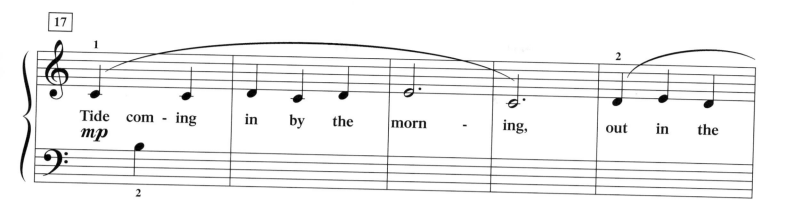

Tide com - ing in by the morn - ing, out in the
mp

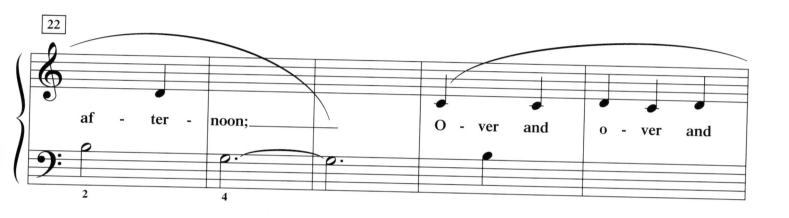

af - ter - noon;_____ O - ver and o - ver and

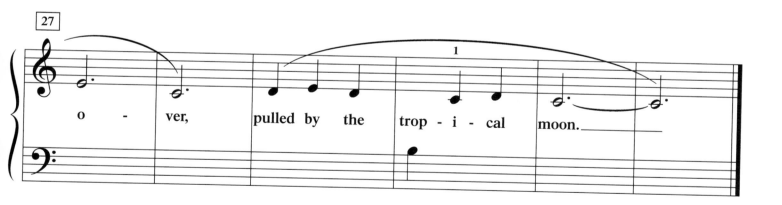

o - ver, pulled by the trop - i - cal moon._____

rit.

Sea Breeze

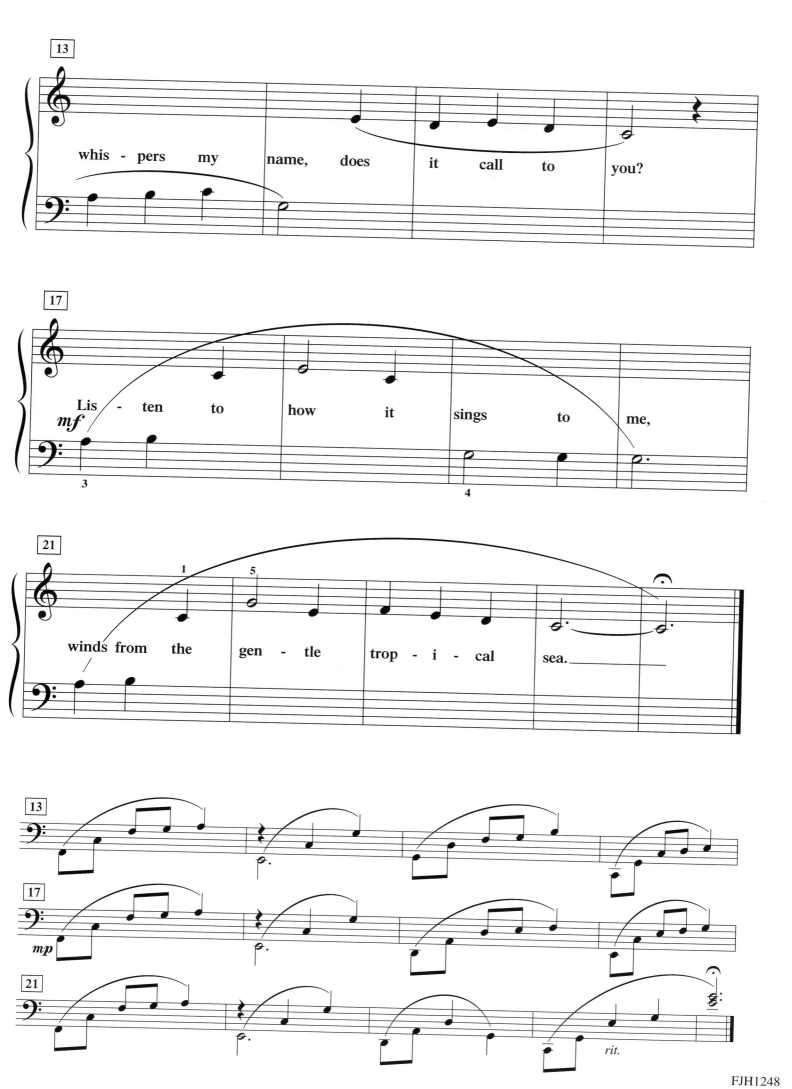

FJH1248

Sails in Sight

Sweet Dreams

Christopher Goldston

Dancing Donkey

Melody Bober

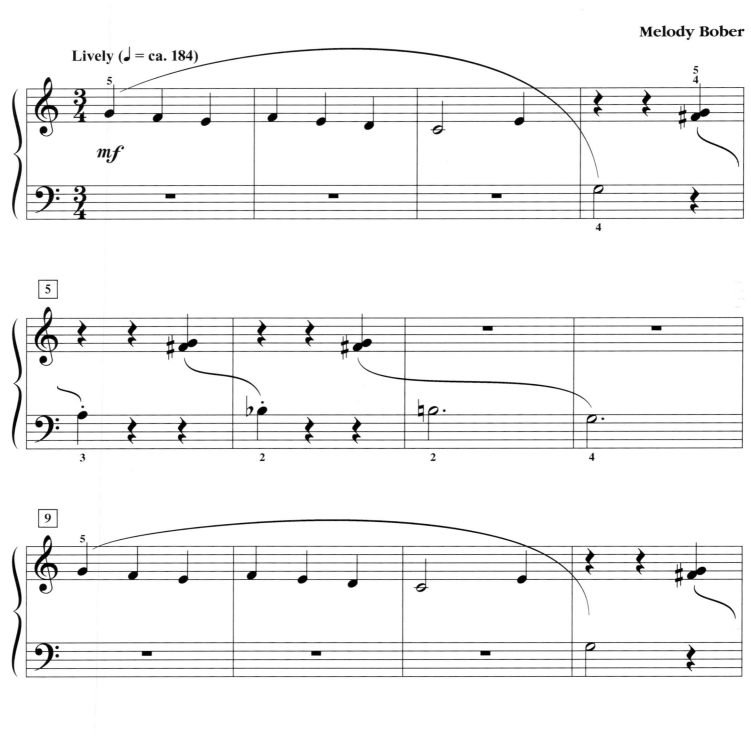

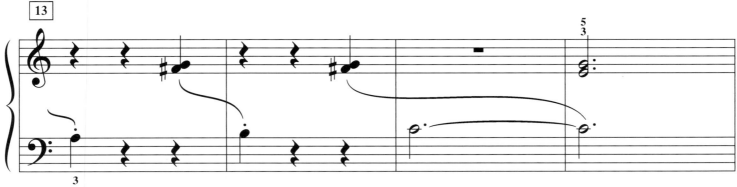

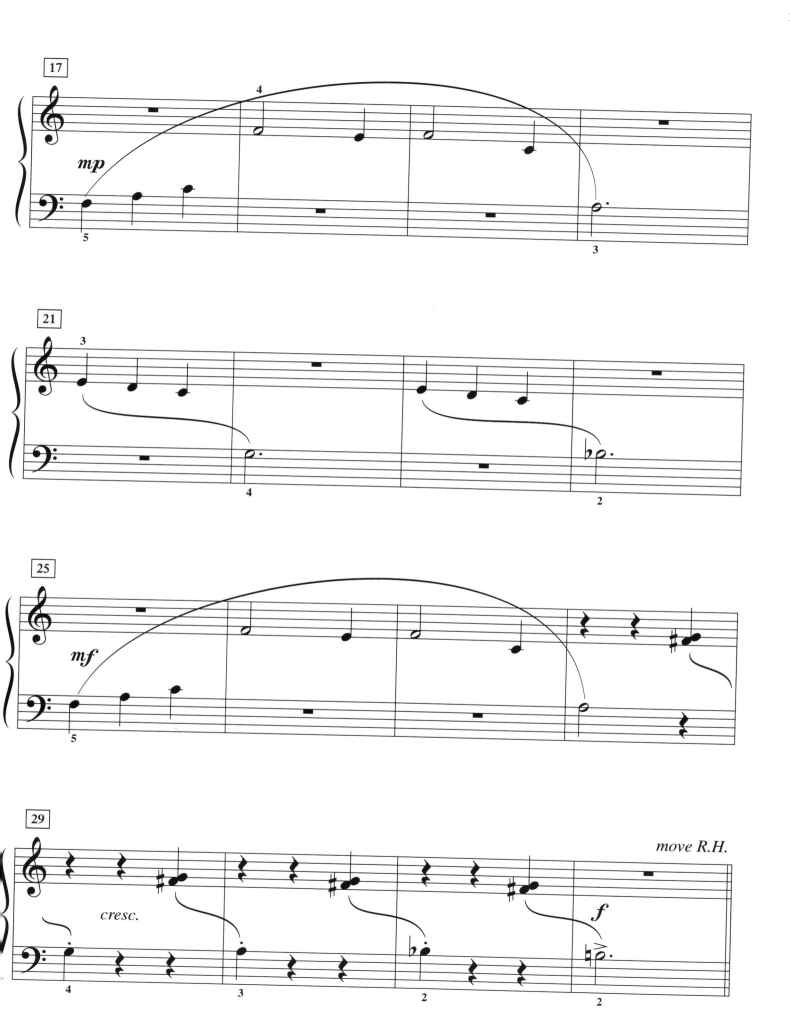

22

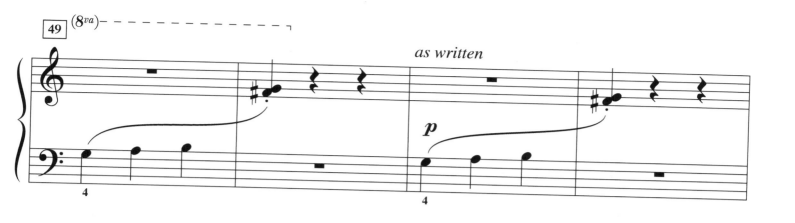

Grandfather's Grandfather Clock

Kevin Olson

move L.H.

move L.H.

The Hermit Crab Cha-Cha

Kevin Olson

Olde English Dance

Melody Bober